Little People, BIG DREAMS™

VINCENT VAN GOGH

Written by
Maria Isabel Sánchez Vegara

Illustrated by
Alette Straathof

Frances Lincoln
Children's Books

Little Vincent was a thoughtful and quiet boy who lived in the Netherlands with his parents and siblings. Vincent was four years older than his brother Theo, but the two shared a very special bond.

When he turned eleven, Vincent was sent to boarding school. There, he missed his long walks in the fields and the company of those he loved most. He was so unhappy that he begged his family to bring him home.

It took him almost four years to get his wish. Soon after, Vincent's uncle found him a job working for a company that sold art. At first, everything went well, but after a while, it became clear that being an art dealer was not for him.

No matter how much he wanted to, Vincent found it difficult to handle his emotions. The dealership tried to help by sending him to a different office. Yet things didn't go well, and Vincent ended up losing his job.

He tried being a teacher, a bookseller, and even a preacher. But despite his best efforts, he seemed to fit in nowhere.

Searching for comfort, Vincent wrote long letters to his beloved brother Theo, telling him of his unhappiness.

Along with his letters, he often included some drawings. Theo found them so fascinating that he told Vincent to try his luck as a painter.

That advice not only changed Vincent's life,
but the history of art forever!

With Theo's support, Vincent practiced day and night and taught himself to be an artist.

For him, painting wasn't about making pretty pictures—it was about showing how he felt. At first, his work was quite dark, like dusty potatoes.

It was when he moved to Paris with Theo that he began to use bright and vibrant colors. Vincent had very little money and couldn't afford to hire models. But that didn't stop him! Instead, he decided to paint himself.

For some time, the city was an exciting source of inspiration. It helped Vincent find his own style of thick, short brushstrokes. But after two years, he longed for peace and quiet and decided to move to the French countryside.

There, he planned to find a big house where he could live and work with other painters. Paul Gauguin was the first to join him, but also the last.

After a heated argument, Vincent was so overwhelmed with emotions that he ended up cutting off his own ear. His mind was unwell, and he needed help.

He agreed to move to a hospital. To calm his mind, Vincent painted the colors of trees, flowers, and the night. But although he put his heart and soul into each piece, he sold very few of the paintings he made during his lifetime.

Still, there was someone who always loved him and treasured his art: his brother. Theo even named his son after Vincent. Filled with pride, Vincent made a beautiful painting for the baby's room.

And though it took time for the world to recognize his talent, little Vincent continued to express his feelings with every single brushstroke. He proved that—even when we feel a bit lost—we can find joy by doing the things we love most.

VINCENT VAN GOGH

(Born 1853 – Died 1890)

1888

1889

Vincent van Gogh grew up in a Dutch village called Zundert with his parents and five siblings. The family took daily walks and enjoyed using their backyard, which grew Vincent's lifelong love of nature. After leaving school early, he went to work at an art dealership and then took jobs as a teacher, bookseller, and preacher. None of these roles were the right fit so, encouraged by his brother Theo, Vincent decided to focus on being an artist. Until then, art had just been a pastime, but he practiced hard and slowly developed his own style. He used vivid colors and thick brushstrokes. He preferred to paint outside and was inspired by people, nature, cities, and his feelings. Vincent's feelings could be very strong. He experienced mental illness at different points in his life. Sometimes he

2005

2021

found the world scary and confusing and he needed help to look after himself. There was not as much knowledge about mental illness as there is now, so it was difficult for Vincent and others to understand what he was experiencing. Yet, among the sad times, there were moments of light. When able, he wrote letters to Theo and kept painting. While in the hospital, he created beautiful pieces, including *Irises*, *The Starry Night,* and A *Wheatfield, with Cypresses*. Although few realized his talent at the time, Vincent's work became widely known and celebrated after his death. Today, his paintings sit in famous galleries, are studied in schools and universities, and inspire people around the world. Vincent's story reminds us that when we find something we love, we should follow it with all our heart.

Want to find out more about **Vincent van Gogh**?

Have a read of this great book:

The Met Vincent van Gogh by Amy Guglielmo and Petra Braun

If you are in Amsterdam, the Netherlands, you could visit the Van Gogh Museum.

Original idea of the series by Maria Isabel Sánchez Vegara, published by Alba Editorial, s.l.u.
"Little People, BIG DREAMS" and "Pequeña & Grande" are trademarks of
Alba Editorial s.l.u. and/or Beautifool Couple S.L.
First Published in the USA in 2024 by Frances Lincoln Children's Books, an imprint of The Quarto Group.
100 Cummings Center, Suite 265D, Beverly, MA 01915, USA. T +1 978-282-9590 **www.Quarto.com**
EEA Representation, WTS Tax d.o.o., Žanova ulica 3, 4000 Kranj, Slovenia. www.wts-tax.si

A CIP record for this book is available from the Library of Congress.
ISBN 978-0-7112-9202-4
Set in Futura BT.

Published by Peter Marley · Designed by Sasha Moxon
Commissioned by Lucy Menzies · Edited by Molly Mead
Production by Robin Boothroyd

Manufactured in Shanghai,China CC122025
5 7 9 8 6 4

Photographic acknowledgments (pages 28-29, from left to right): 1. Self Portrait 1888 Vincent van Gogh 1853 - 1890 Dutch Netherlands Post Impressionism © Peter Horree via Alamy Stock Photo. 2. Vincent van Gogh Self Portrait (719161) © Historic Images via Alamy Stock Photo. 3. Vincent Van Gogh's painting "Self Portrait with a Straw Hat" is displayed at the exhibit "Vincent van Gogh: The Drawings" during a press preview at the Metropolitan Museum of Art October 11, 2005 in New York City. The major exhibition is the first in the U.S. to focus on Van Gogh's drawings and will be open to the public October 18 through December 31, 2005 © Photo Mario Tama via Getty Images. 4. Van Gogh Self Portraits at the immersive Van Gogh Exhibit in Scottsdale, AZ © Martin Konopacki via Alamy Stock Photo.

Collect the *Little People,* **BIG DREAMS**™ series:

FRIDA KAHLO
COCO CHANEL
MAYA ANGELOU
AMELIA EARHART
AGATHA CHRISTIE
MARIE CURIE
ROSA PARKS
AUDREY HEPBURN
EMMELINE PANKHURST 
ELLA FITZGERALD
ADA LOVELACE
JANE AUSTEN
GEORGIA O'KEEFFE
HARRIET TUBMAN
ANNE FRANK
MOTHER TERESA
JOSEPHINE BAKER
L. M. MONTGOMERY 
JANE GOODALL
SIMONE DE BEAUVOIR
MUHAMMAD ALI
STEPHEN HAWKING
MARIA MONTESSORI
VIVIENNE WESTWOOD
MAHATMA GANDHI
DAVID BOWIE
WILMA RUDOLPH 
DOLLY PARTON
BRUCE LEE
RUDOLF NUREYEV
ZAHA HADID
MARY SHELLEY
MARTIN LUTHER KING JR.
DAVID ATTENBOROUGH
ASTRID LINDGREN
EVONNE GOOLAGONG 
BOB DYLAN
ALAN TURING
BILLIE JEAN KING
GRETA THUNBERG
JESSE OWENS
JEAN-MICHEL BASQUIAT
ARETHA FRANKLIN
CORAZON AQUINO
PELÉ 
RNEST SHACKLETON
STEVE JOBS
AYRTON SENNA
LOUISE BOURGEOIS
ELTON JOHN
JOHN LENNON
PRINCE
CHARLES DARWIN
CAPTAIN TOM MOORE 
HANS CHRISTIAN ANDERSEN
STEVIE WONDER
MEGAN RAPINOE
MARY ANNING
MALALA YOUSAFZAI
ANDY WARHOL
RUPAUL
MICHELLE OBAMA
MINDY KALING

IRIS APFEL

ROSALIND FRANKLIN

RUTH BADER GINSBURG

MARILYN MONROE

KAMALA HARRIS

ALBERT EINSTEIN

CHARLES DICKENS

YOKO ONO

MICHAEL JORDAN

NELSON MANDELA
PABLO PICASSO
AMANDA GORMAN
GLORIA STEINEM
FLORENCE NIGHTINGALE
HARRY HOUDINI
J.R.R. TOLKIEN
ELVIS PRESLEY
NEIL ARMSTRONG
ALEXANDER VON HUMBOLDT
NIKOLA TESLA
WILMA MANKILLER
MARCUS RASHFORD
LAVERNE COX
MAE JEMISON
DWAYNE JOHNSON
HELEN KELLER
ANNA PAVLOVA
QUEEN ELIZABETH
TERRY FOX
HEDY LAMARR
SHAKIRA
FREDDIE MERCURY
LEWIS HAMILTON
LOUIS PASTEUR
PRINCESS DIANA
DAVID HOCKNEY
VANESSA NAKATE
OLIVE MORRIS
KING CHARLES
MOZART
STEVE IRWIN
JÜRGEN KLOPP
LEO MESSI
SALLY RIDE
TENZING NORGAY
KYLIE MINOGUE
BEYONCÉ
TAYLOR SWIFT
RAFA NADAL
USAIN BOLT
SIMONE BILES
STAN LEE
LEONARD COHEN
VINCENT VAN GOGH
MARY KOM
SALVADOR DALÍ
ANTOINE DE SAINT-EXUPÉRY
DAVID BECKHAM
KATHERINE JOHNSON
PATRICK MAHOMES
YAYOI KUSAMA
ROALD DAHL
HARRY STYLES
WILLIAM KAMKWAMBA
MARY EARPS
YVES SAINT LAURENT
BOB MARLEY
VIRGINIA WOOLF
LUDWIG VAN BEETHOVEN
LOUIS BRAILLE
STEVEN SPIELBERG
CHRIS HOY
MIKAELA SHIFFRIN
BEATRIX POTTER
RIHANNA
WILLIAM SHAKESPEARE
OPRAH WINFREY
Scan the QR code for free activit
sheets, teachers' notes and mor
information about the series at
www.littlepeoplebigdreams.com